The Complete Elegies, the Six Sonatinas

and Other Original Works for Solo Piano

Ferruccio Busoni

DOVER PUBLICATIONS, INC.

Mineola, New York

Bibliographical Note

This Dover edition, first published in 1996, is a new compilation of Ferruccio Busoni's works for solo piano originally published separately. *Stücke*, Op. 33b, and *Sonatina seconda* were originally published in unidentified authoritative editions, n.d. All other works in this compilation were originally published by Breitkopf & Härtel, Wiesbaden, under the following Edition Breitkopf numbers, listed in numerical order: *Fantasia nach Johann Sebastian Bach:* No. 3054, n.d., designated "Kindermann-Verz[eichnis] 253"; *Fantasia Contrappuntistica*, No. 3491, n.d.; *Sonatina ad usum infantis pro clavicimbalo composita:* No. 4836, 1916; *Indianisches Tagebuch, Erstes Buch / Vier Klavierstudien über Motive der Rothäute Amerikas:* No. 4837, 1916; *Sonatina in diem nativitatis Christi 1917:* No. 5071, n.d.; *Sonatina brevis in Signo Joannis Sebastiani Magni:* No. 5093, 1919; *Kammer-Fantasie über Bizets Carmen:* No. 5186, n.d.; *Elegien / Sieben neue Klavierstücke:* No. 5214, n.d.; and *Sonatina* [No. 1]: No. 8146, n.d.

The Dover edition adds a composite table of contents with new English translations, new headings throughout, and translations of German performance notes in the scores. The quotation on page 35 appeared in *The New Grove Dictionary of Music and Musicians*, Macmillan Publishers Limited, London, 1980: Vol. 3. The note "Hier endet . . ." on page 122 originally appeared in a different edition of the *Fantasia Contrappuntistica*. We are grateful to pianist Mark Riggleman for his assistance in obtaining a copy of the *Kammer-Fantasie* for this edition.

International Standard Book Number: 0-486-29386-6

Manufactured in the United States of America
Dover Publications, Inc., 31 East 2nd Street, Mineola, N.Y. 11501

CONTENTS

STÜCKE
Pieces

Op. 33b (1896)

To Mr. Max Reger

Schwermut
Melancholy

Stücke, Op. 33b, No. 1 (1896)

[The downstemmed notes are for the left hand, the upstemmed notes for the right.]

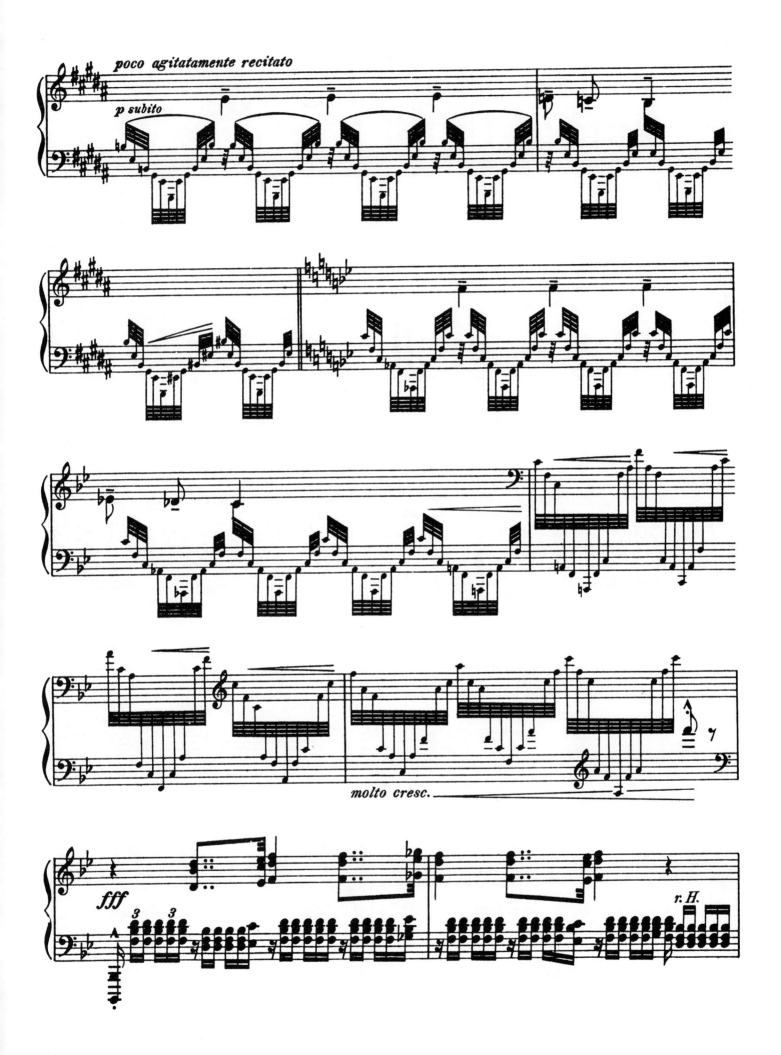

Frohsinn
Gaiety

Stücke, Op. 33b, No. 2 (1896)

Tempo di Valse, elegante e vivace.

Poco a poco più stretto e più forte.

Scherzino
Little scherzo

Stücke, Op. 33b, No. 3 (1896)

To Mrs. Isabella S. Gardner in Boston

Fantasia in modo antico
Fantasy in olden style

Stücke, Op. 33b, No. 4 (1896)

Allegro risoluto.

Finnische Ballade
Finnish ballad

Stücke, Op. 33b, No. 5 (1896)

"Exeunt omnes"
"All depart"
(Schluss-Musik • *Recessional Music*)

Stücke, Op. 33b, No. 6 (1896)

Pomposo marziale e vivace.

ELEGIEN

Sieben neue Klavierstücke

Elegies: Seven new piano pieces

(1907)

"I have expressed the very essence of myself in the *Elegies* . . .
[These pieces were not designed to] overthrow something exist-
ing but to recreate something that exists . . . Everything experi-
mental from the beginning of the twentieth century should be
used, incorporated in the coming finality."

Ferruccio Busoni, 1907

Nach der Wendung

After the turning

en affaiblissant [growing weaker]

All'Italia!
(in modo napolitano)
To Italy! (in Neapolitan style)

No. 2 of *Elegien* (1907)

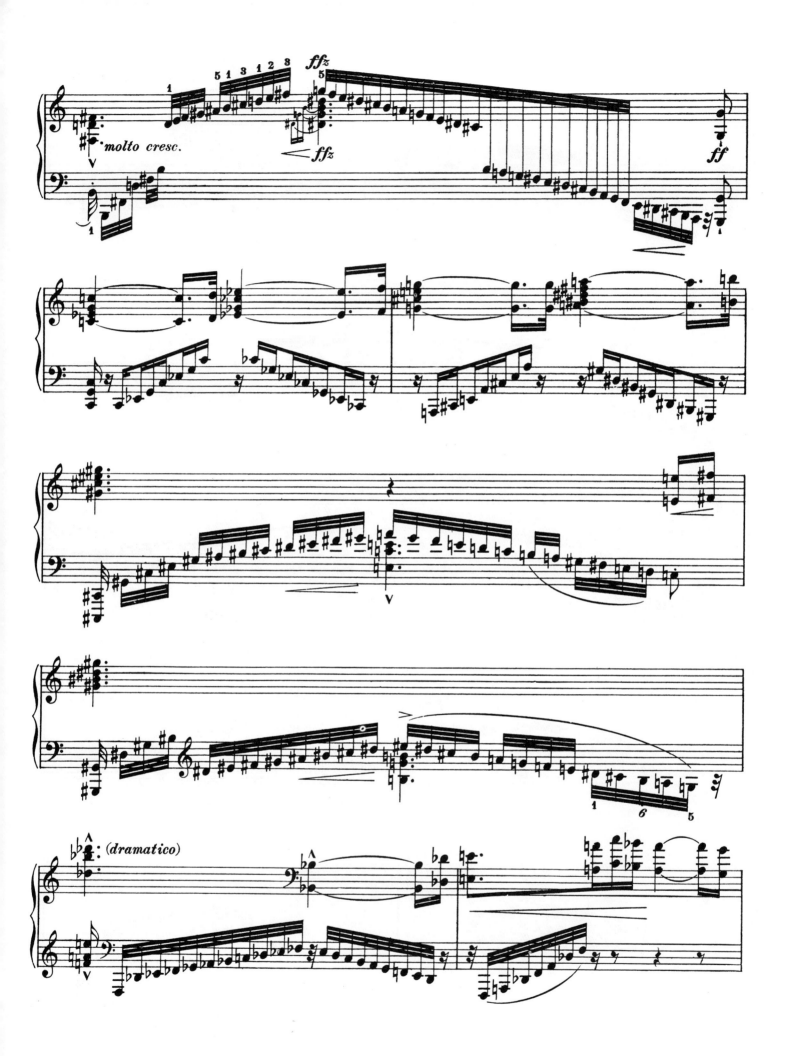

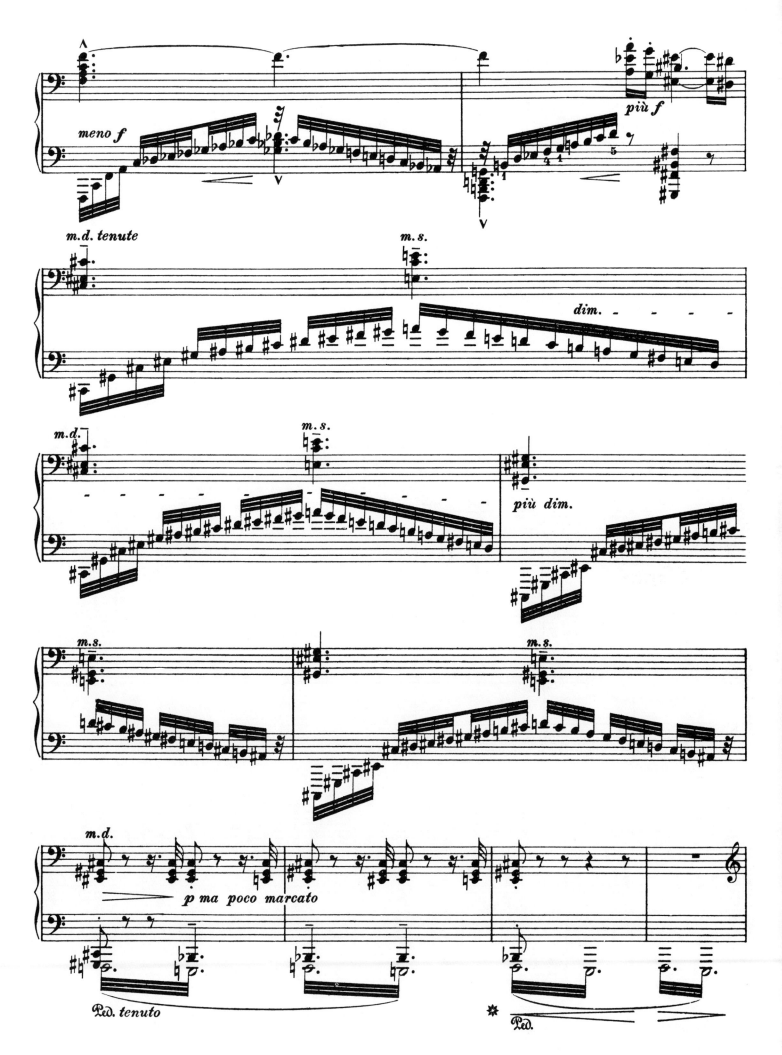

"Meine Seele bangt und hofft zu Dir"

"My soul fears and hopes in You"

(Chorale prelude)

No. 3 of *Elegien* (1907)

54

flehend
(implorando)
mf

sehr ausdrucksvoll, mit unterdrückter Empfindung
(molto espressivo, ma consentimento soppresso)

Senza Ped.

p eguale

p

dolce

ansioso

p

"Meine Seele"

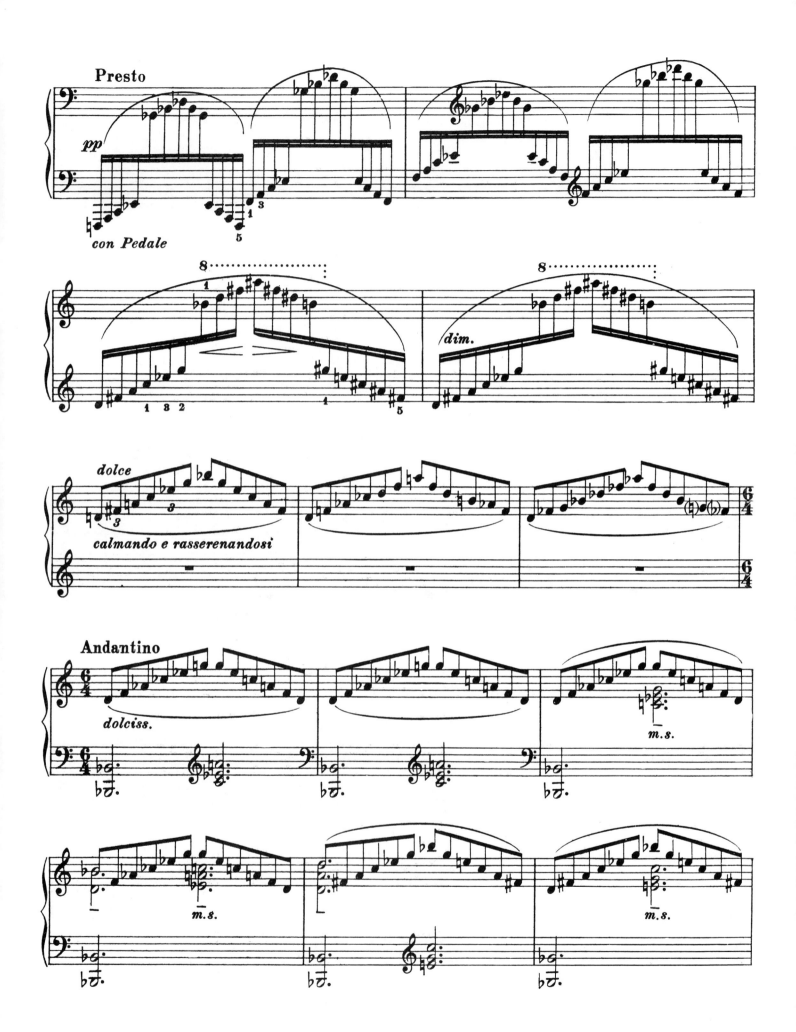

"Meine Seele"

"Meine Seele"

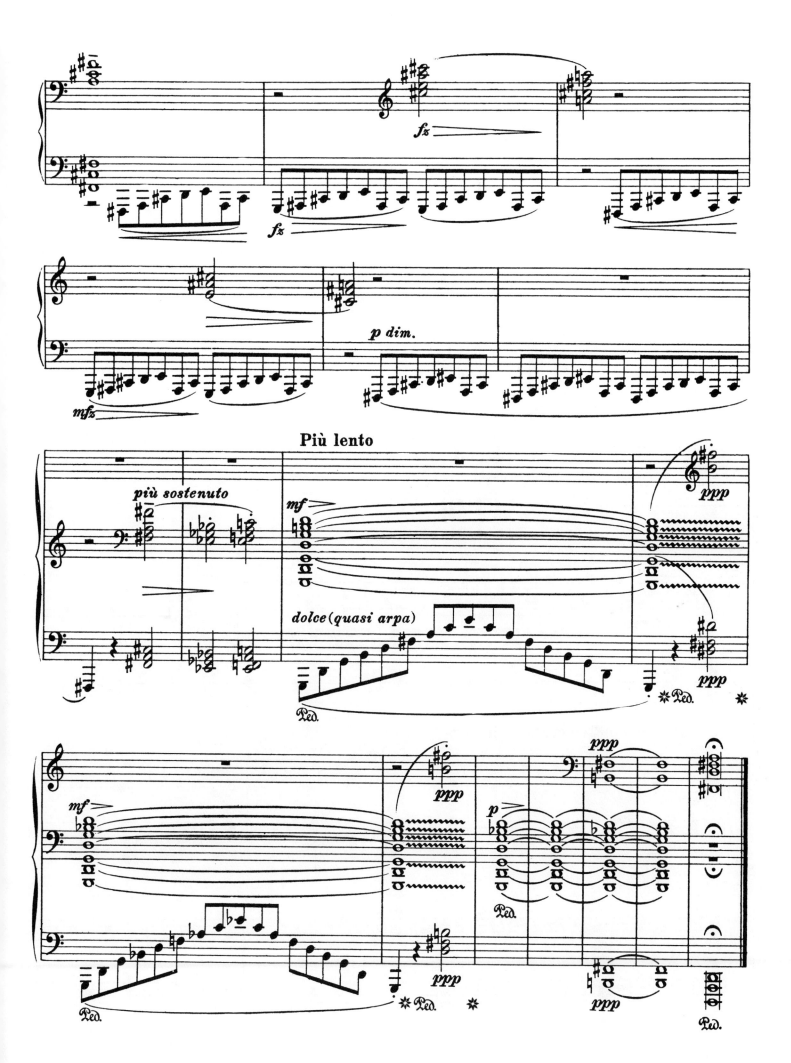

Più lento

To Michael von Zadora

Turandots Frauengemach

Turandot's room

(Intermezzo)

No. 4 of *Elegien* (1907)

Andantino sereno

dolce assai

sempre i due Pedali
tenuti fino al ⊕

Più vivo e distaccato e ritmato

To O'Neil Phillips

Die Nächtlichen
The Nocturnals

(Waltz)

Schnell, flüchtig und verschleiert
Rapido, fuggevole e velato

Un poco più tranquillo
dolcissimo

trillo

Erscheinung

Apparition

(Nocturne)

No. 6 of *Elegien* (1907)

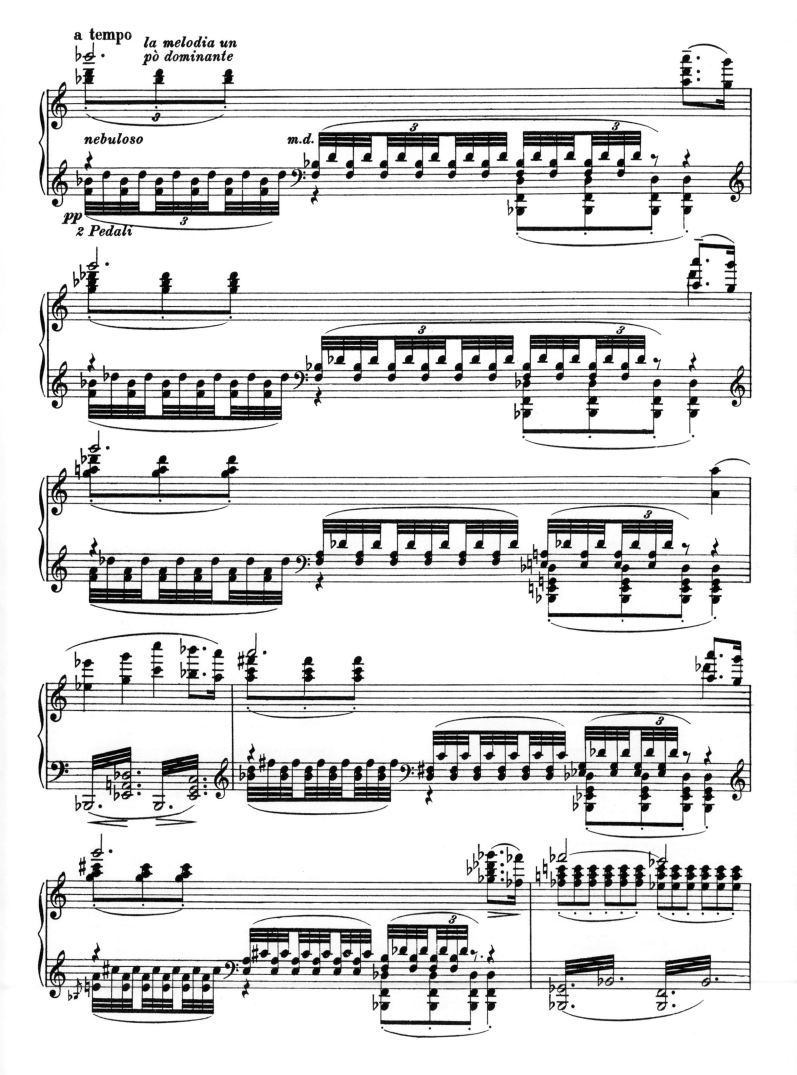

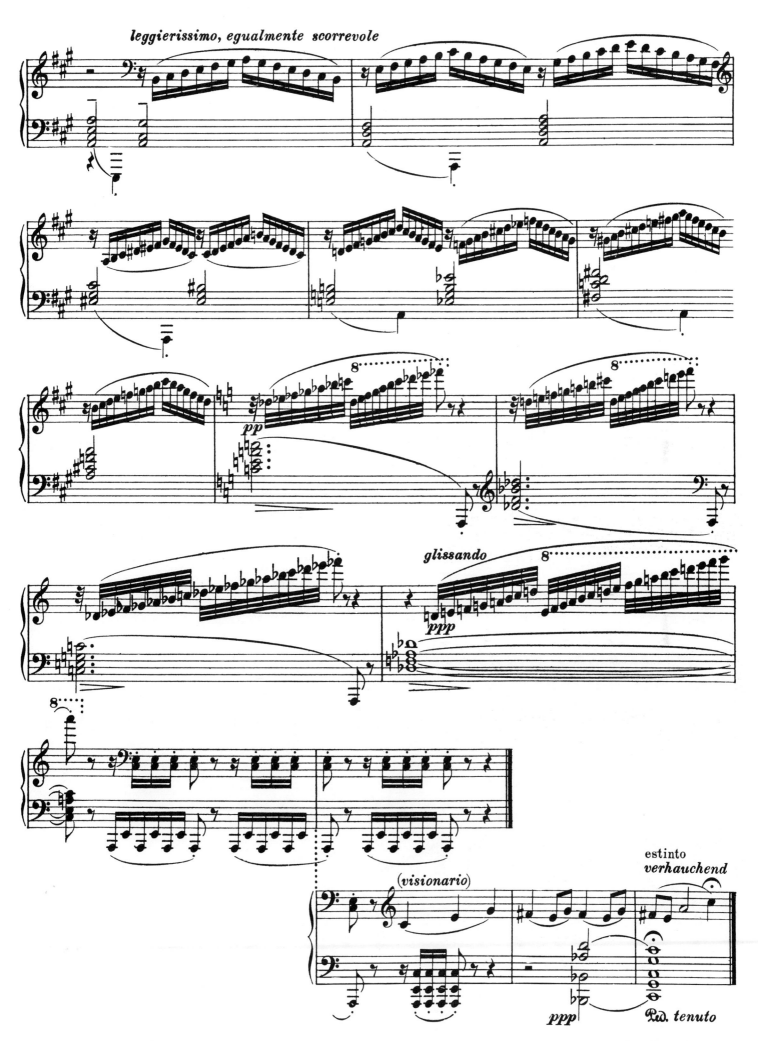

Berceuse
Lullaby

No. 7 of *Elegien* (1907)

Andantino calmo

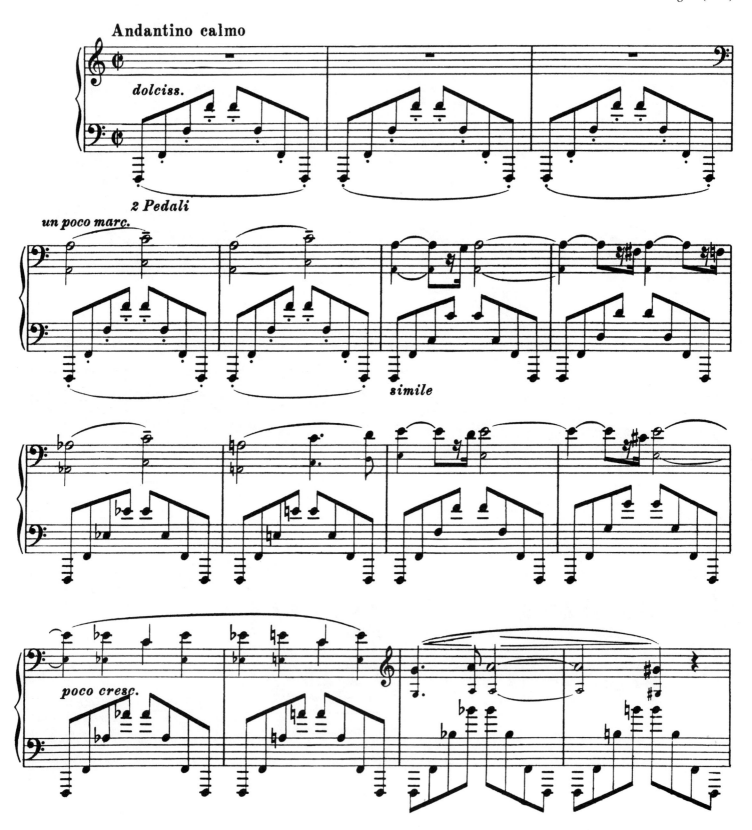

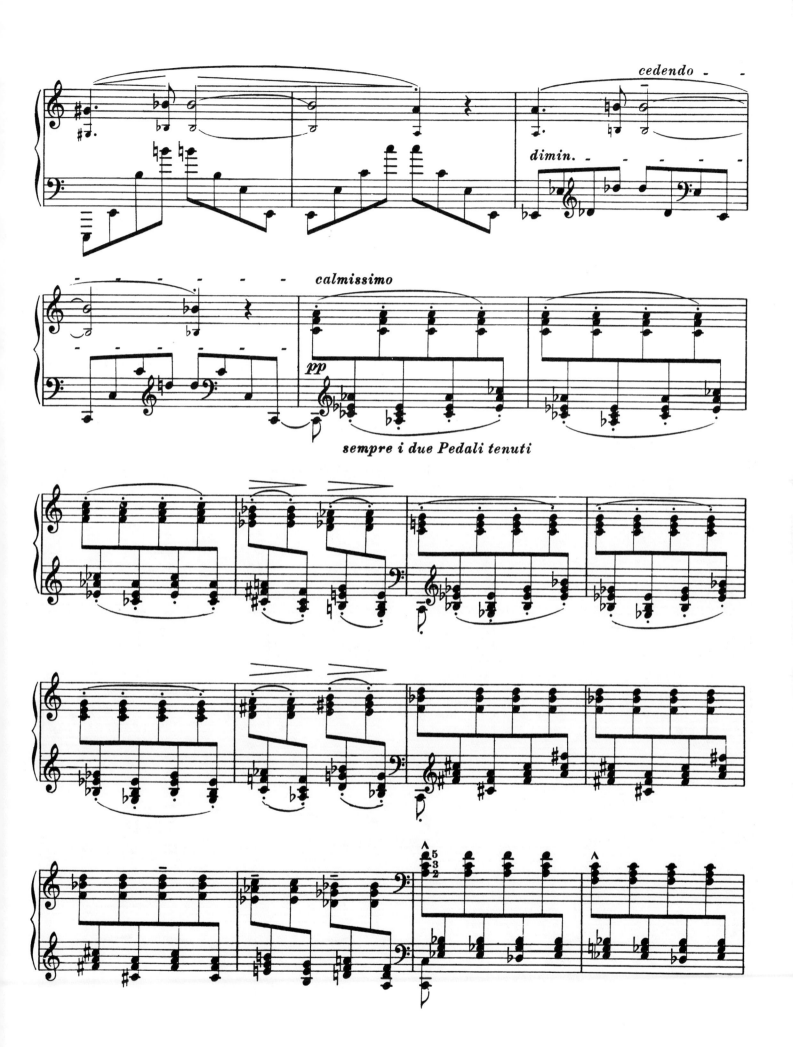

TWO FANTASIES

(1909 / 1912)

Fantasia nach Johann Sebastian Bach

Fantasy after J. S. Bach

(1909)

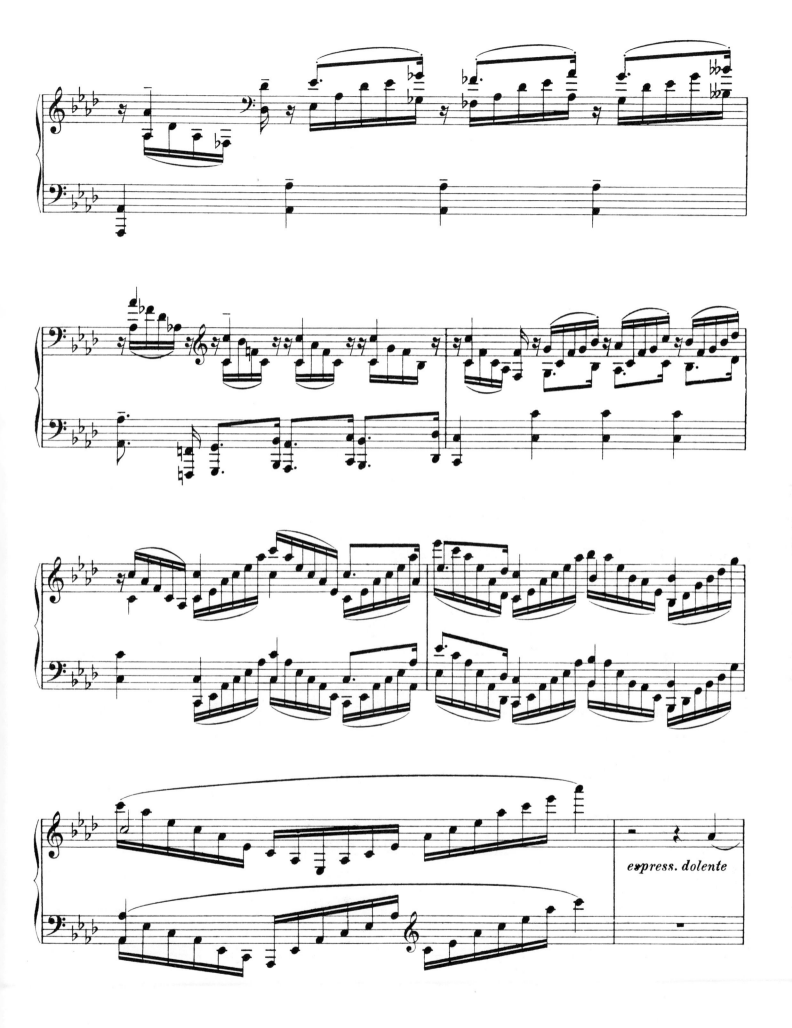

Fantasia nach J. S. Bach

Andante, quasi Adagio
il tutto sottovoce

molto sostenuto
il Basso

To Wilhelm Middelschulte, Master of Counterpoint

Fantasia Contrappuntistica
Contrapuntal fantasy
(3rd, final version, 1912)

Preludio corale

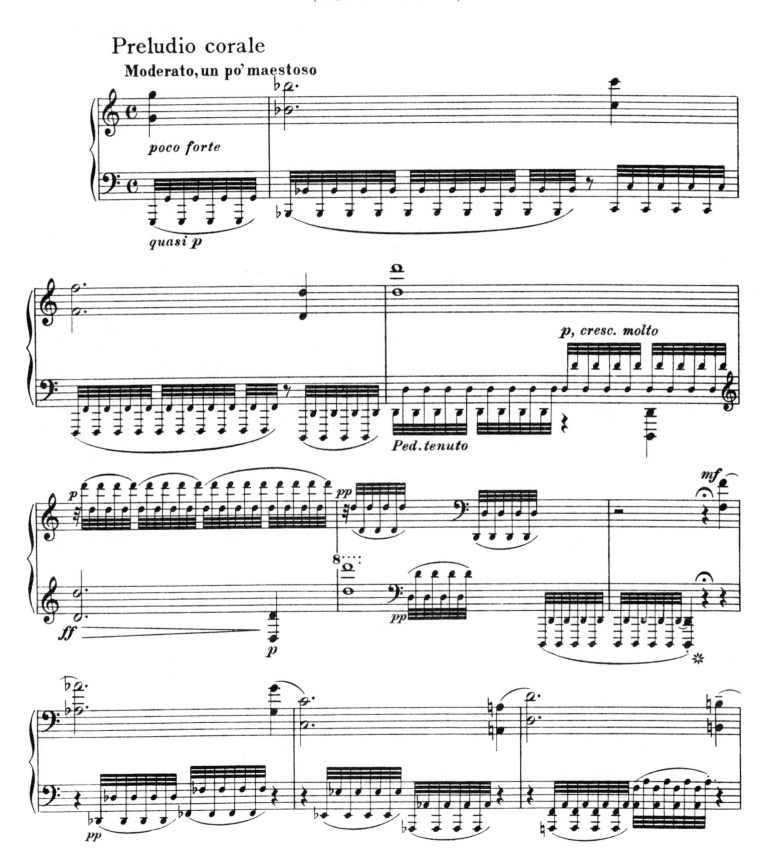

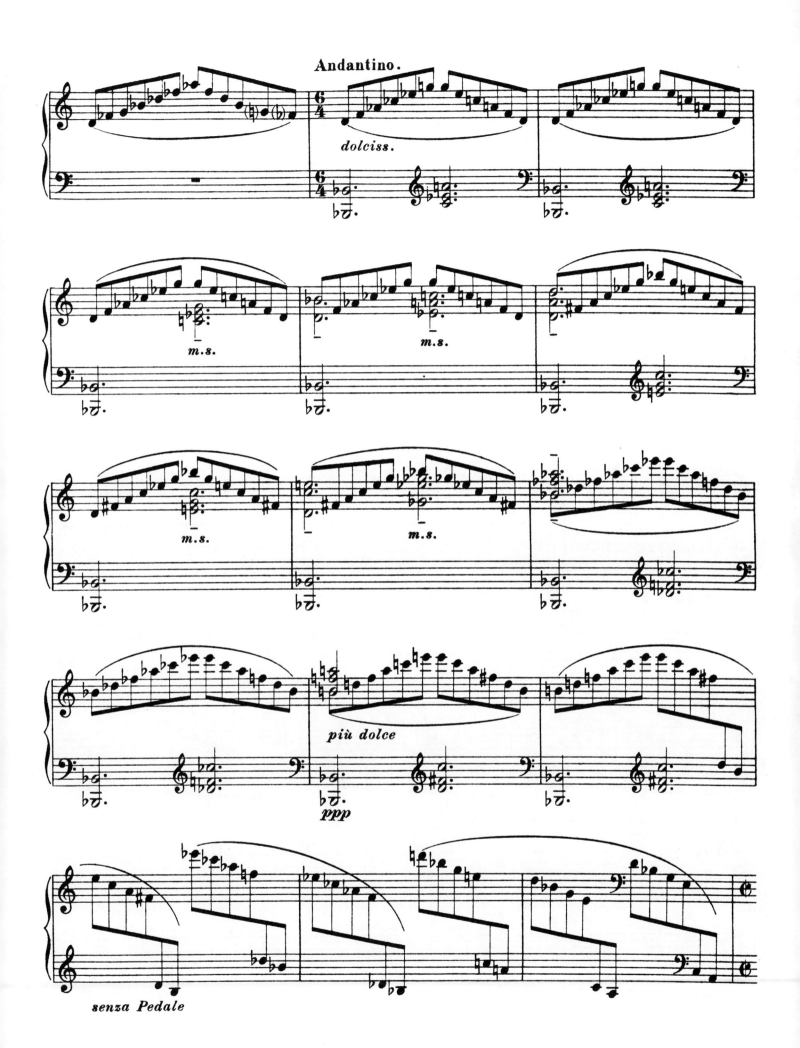

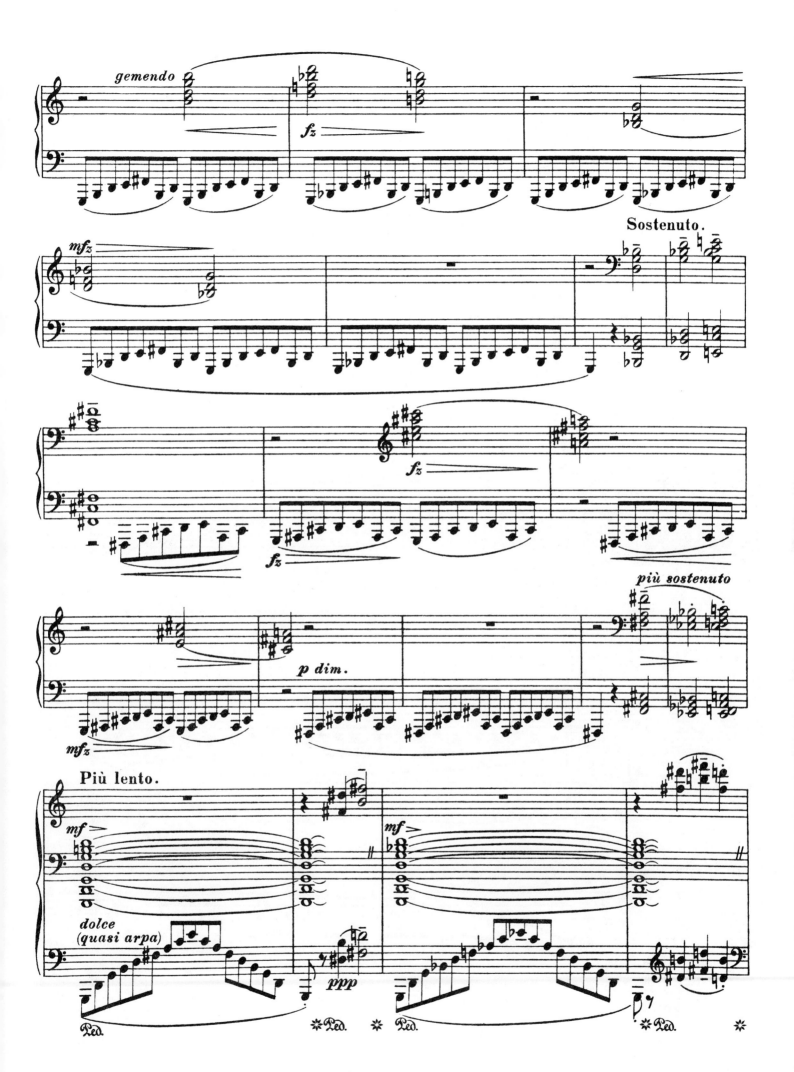

Fuga I.

Fuga II.

Fuga III.

↓ ["Hier endet Bachs Fragment"] [Here ends Bach's fragment]

Intermezzo.

(più tranquillo e misticamente)

Variazione I.

A tempo, tranquillo molto
dolce, cantabile

Variazione III.

Fuga IV.

NB. Siehe Anhang. [see Supplement, p. 144]

Fantasia Contrappuntistica 137

Stretta

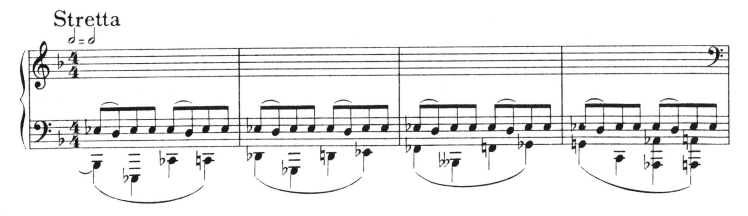

140   Fantasia Contrappuntistica

Supplement to the
Fantasia Contrappuntistica

Die Originalfassung bringt an dieser Stelle noch die folgende Durchführung, die der Komponist bei dem öffentlichen Vortrag übergeht:
[At this point the original version includes the following development, which the composer omits in public performance:]

INDIANISCHES TAGEBUCH

Erstes Buch

Vier Klavierstudien über Motive der Rothäute Amerikas

Indian Diary (Book 1, 1915): Four piano studies on American Indian Motifs

To Helen Luise Birch

Indianisches Tagebuch
Indian Diary

(Book 1, 1915)

1.

Allegretto affettuoso, un poco agitato

Indianisches Tagebuch
Indian Diary

(Book 1, 1915)

2.

Indianisches Tagebuch
Indian Diary
(Book 1, 1915)

3.

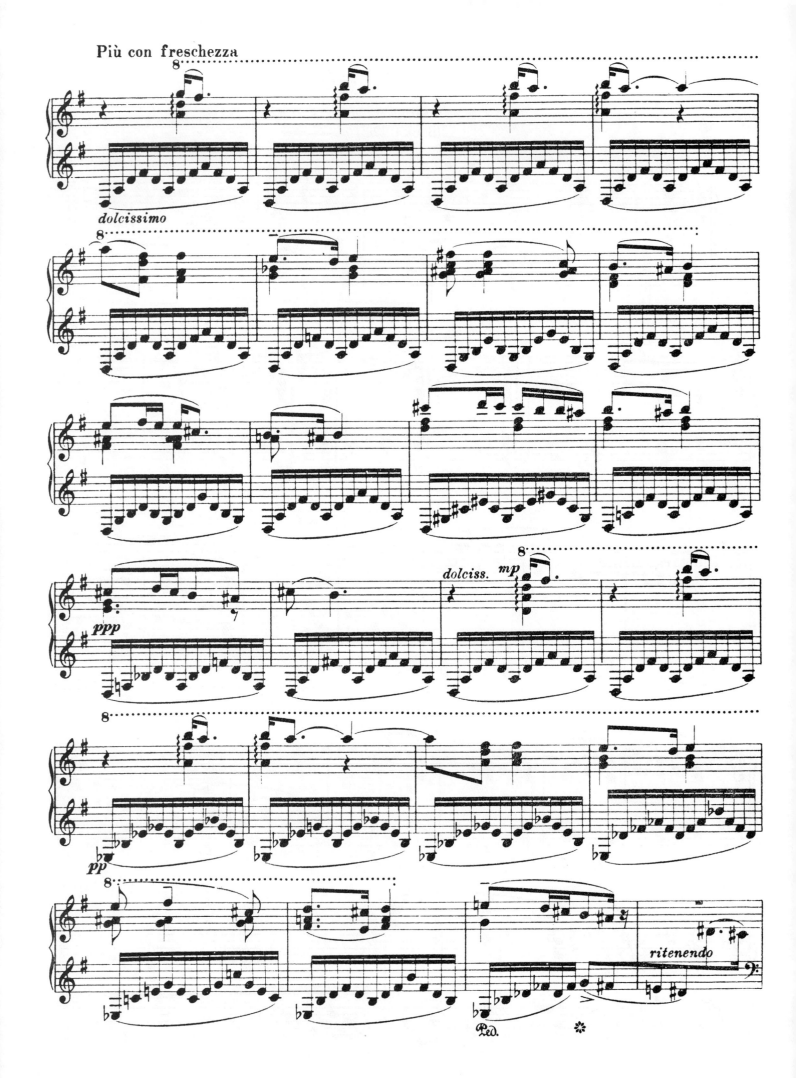

Indianisches Tagebuch
Indian Diary
(Book 1, 1915)

4.

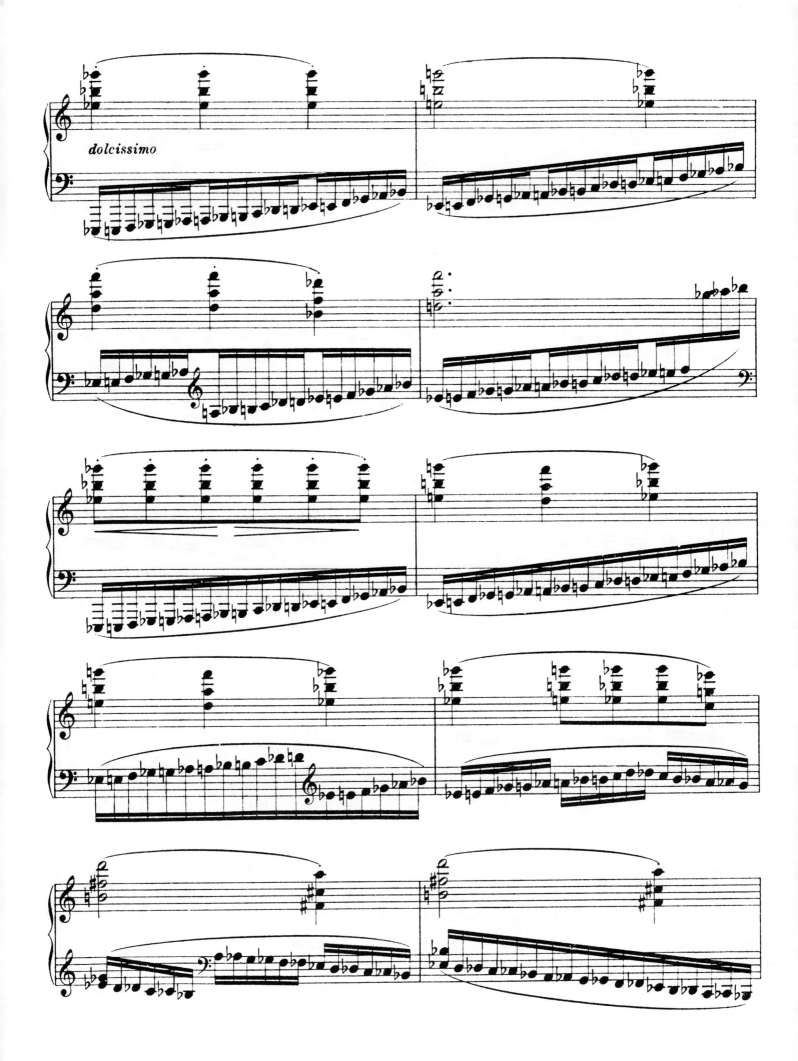

SIX SONATINAS

(1910–20)

Sonatina [No. 1]

(1910)

Semplice, commovente

(mezza voce)

dolce

fz

pp

Allegretto elegante

Teneramente, come da principio

To Mark Hambourg

Sonatina Seconda
Second sonatina

(1912)

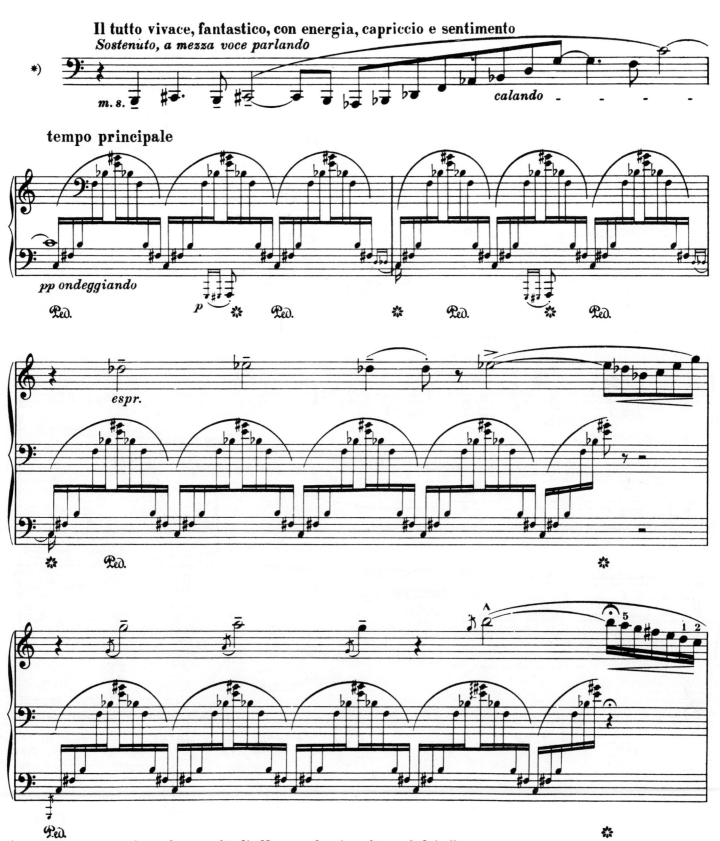

Un poco più sostenuto e posato

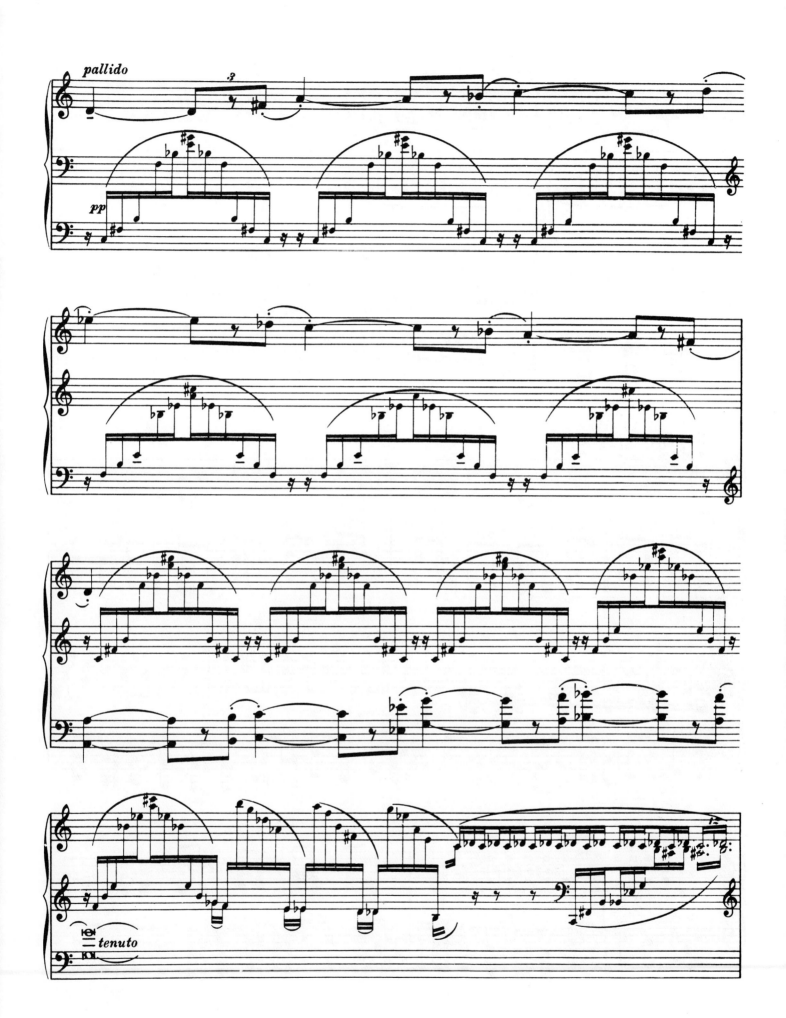

poco a poco più andando

Sostenuto, un poco marziale (quasi ♩ = ♪)

mezzo piano

8ª basso

sempre più piano

estinto

Sonatina [No. 3]
ad usum infantis Madeline M.* Americanae
pro Clavicimbalo composita

...for the use of the American "princess" Madeline M.,
written for the piano

(1916)

2. Andantino melancolico

meno *f e legato*

quasi forte, chiamando

teneramente

3. Vivace (alla Marcia)

più apertamente

cresc.

To Benvenuto

Sonatina [No. 4]
in diem nativitatis Christi MCMXVII
...on the day of Christ's birth, 1917

204

con 2 Pedali continuamente

Moderatamente vivace

To Philipp Jarnach

Sonatina brevis
[Sonatina No. 5]
'in Signo Joannis Sebastiani Magni'

Short sonatina 'in the sign of the great Johann Sebastian'—
a free imitation of Bach's Little Fantasy and Fugue in D Minor

(1919)

Tema dell' Andante

As a token of esteem and gratitude,
to Monsieur Tauber,* Paris, March 1920

Kammer-Fantasie
über Bizets "Carmen"
[Sonatina No. 6]

[*Chamber-Fantasy on Bizet's "Carmen"*]

(1920)

*possibly the celebrated tenor Richard Tauber who, though not generally associated with *Carmen*, counted Don José
among his theatrical roles

END OF EDITION

Dover Piano and Keyboard Editions

Albeniz, Isaac, IBERIA AND ESPAÑA: Two Complete Works for Solo Piano. Spanish composer's greatest piano works in authoritative editions. Includes the popular "Tango." 192pp. 9 x 12. 0-486-25367-8

Bach, Johann Sebastian, COMPLETE KEYBOARD TRANSCRIPTIONS OF CONCERTOS BY BAROQUE COMPOSERS. Sixteen concertos by Vivaldi, Telemann and others, transcribed for solo keyboard instruments. Bach-Gesellschaft edition. 128pp. 9⅜ x 12¼. 0-486-25529-8

Bach, Johann Sebastian, COMPLETE PRELUDES AND FUGUES FOR ORGAN. All 25 of Bach's complete sets of preludes and fugues (i.e. compositions written as pairs), from the authoritative Bach-Gesellschaft edition. 168pp. 8⅜ x 11. 0-486-24816-X

Bach, Johann Sebastian, ITALIAN CONCERTO, CHROMATIC FANTASIA AND FUGUE AND OTHER WORKS FOR KEYBOARD. Sixteen of Bach's best-known, most-performed and most-recorded works for the keyboard, reproduced from the authoritative Bach-Gesellschaft edition. 112pp. 9 x 12. 0-486-25387-2

Bach, Johann Sebastian, KEYBOARD MUSIC. Bach-Gesellschaft edition. For harpsichord, piano, other keyboard instruments. English Suites, French Suites, Six Partitas, Goldberg Variations, Two-Part Inventions, Three-Part Sinfonias. 312pp. 8⅛ x 11. 0-486-22360-4

Bach, Johann Sebastian, ORGAN MUSIC. Bach-Gesellschaft edition. 93 works. 6 Trio Sonatas, German Organ Mass, Orgelbüchlein, Six Schubler Chorales, 18 Choral Preludes. 357pp. 8⅛ x 11. 0-486-22359-0

Bach, Johann Sebastian, TOCCATAS, FANTASIAS, PASSACAGLIA AND OTHER WORKS FOR ORGAN. Over 20 best-loved works including Toccata and Fugue in D Minor, BWV 565; Passacaglia and Fugue in C Minor, BWV 582, many more. Bach-Gesellschaft edition. 176pp. 9 x 12. 0-486-25403-8

Bach, Johann Sebastian, TWO- AND THREE-PART INVENTIONS. Reproduction of original autograph ms. Edited by Eric Simon. 62pp. 8⅛ x 11. 0-486-21982-8

Bach, Johann Sebastian, THE WELL-TEMPERED CLAVIER: Books I and II, Complete. All 48 preludes and fugues in all major and minor keys. Authoritative Bach-Gesellschaft edition. Explanation of ornaments in English, tempo indications, music corrections. 208pp. 9⅜ x 12¼. 0-486-24532-2

Bartók, Béla, PIANO MUSIC OF BÉLA BARTÓK, Series I. New, definitive Archive Edition incorporating composer's corrections. Includes *Funeral March* from *Kossuth*, Fourteen Bagatelles, Bartók's break to modernism. 167pp. 9 x 12. (Available in U.S. only) 0-486-24108-4

Bartók, Béla, PIANO MUSIC OF BÉLA BARTÓK, Series II. Second in the Archive Edition incorporating composer's corrections. 85 short pieces *For Children,* Two Elegies, Two Romanian Dances, etc. 192pp. 9 x 12. (Available in U.S. only) 0-486-24109-2

Beethoven, Ludwig van, BAGATELLES, RONDOS AND OTHER SHORTER WORKS FOR PIANO. Most popular and most performed shorter works, including Rondo a capriccio in G and Andante in F. Breitkopf & Härtel edition. 128pp. 9⅜ x 12¼. 0-486-25392-9

Beethoven, Ludwig van, COMPLETE PIANO SONATAS. All sonatas in fine Schenker edition, with fingering, analytical material. One of best modern editions. 615pp. 9 x 12. Two-vol. set. 0-486-23134-8, 0-486-23135-6

Beethoven, Ludwig van, COMPLETE VARIATIONS FOR SOLO PIANO, Ludwig van Beethoven. Contains all 21 sets of Beethoven's piano variations, including the extremely popular *Diabelli Variations, Op. 120.* 240pp. 9⅜ x 12¼. 0-486-25188-8

Beethoven, Ludwig van, BEETHOVEN MASTERPIECES FOR SOLO PIANO: 25 Works. Twenty-five popular pieces include the Sonata in C-sharp Minor, Op. 27, No. 2 ("Moonlight"); Sonata in D Minor, Op. 31, No. 2 ("Tempest"); 32 Variations in C Minor; Andante in F Major; Rondo Capriccio, Op. 129; Fantasia, Op. 77; and popular bagatelles, rondos, minuets, and other works. 160pp. 9 x 12. 0-486-43570-9

Blesh, Rudi (ed.), CLASSIC PIANO RAGS. Best ragtime music (1897–1922) by Scott Joplin, James Scott, Joseph F. Lamb, Tom Turpin, nine others. 364pp. 9 x 12. Introduction by Blesh. 0-486-20469-3

Brahms, Johannes, COMPLETE SHORTER WORKS FOR SOLO PIANO. All solo music not in other two volumes. Waltzes, Scherzo in E Flat Minor, Eight Pieces, Rhapsodies, Fantasies, Intermezzi, etc. Vienna Gesellschaft der Musikfreunde. 180pp. 9 x 12. 0-486-22651-4

Brahms, Johannes, COMPLETE SONATAS AND VARIATIONS FOR SOLO PIANO. All sonatas, five variations on themes from Schumann, Paganini, Handel, etc. Vienna Gesellschaft der Musikfreunde edition. 178pp. 9 x 12. 0-486-22650-6

Brahms, Johannes, COMPLETE TRANSCRIPTIONS, CADENZAS AND EXERCISES FOR SOLO PIANO. Vienna Gesellschaft der Musikfreunde edition, vol. 15. Studies after Chopin, Weber, Bach; gigues, sarabandes; 10 Hungarian dances, etc. 178pp. 9 x 12. 0-486-22652-2

Byrd, William, MY LADY NEVELLS BOOKE OF VIRGINAL MUSIC. 42 compositions in modern notation from 1591 ms. For any keyboard instrument. 245pp. 8⅛ x 11. 0-486-22246-2

Chopin, Frédéric, COMPLETE BALLADES, IMPROMPTUS AND SONATAS. The four Ballades, four Impromptus and three Sonatas. Authoritative Mikuli edition. 192pp. 9 x 12. 0-486-24164-5

Chopin, Frédéric, COMPLETE MAZURKAS, Frédéric Chopin. 51 best-loved compositions, reproduced directly from the authoritative Kistner edition edited by Carl Mikuli. 160pp. 9 x 12. 0-486-25548-4

Chopin, Frédéric, COMPLETE PRELUDES AND ETUDES FOR SOLO PIANO. All 25 Preludes and all 27 Etudes by greatest piano music composer. Authoritative Mikuli edition. 192pp. 9 x 12. 0-486-24052-5

Chopin, Frédéric, FANTASY IN F MINOR, BARCAROLLE, BERCEUSE AND OTHER WORKS FOR SOLO PIANO. 15 works, including one of the greatest of the Romantic period, the Fantasy in F Minor, Op. 49, reprinted from the authoritative German edition prepared by Chopin's student, Carl Mikuli. 224pp. 8⅜ x 11¼. 0-486-25950-1

Chopin, Frédéric, CHOPIN MASTERPIECES FOR SOLO PIANO: 46 Works. Includes Ballade No. 1 in G Minor, Berceuse, 3 ecossaises, 5 etudes, Fantaisie-Impromptu, Marche Funèbre, 8 mazurkas, 7 nocturnes, 3 polonaises, 9 preludes, Scherzo No. 2 in B-flat Minor, and 6 waltzes. Authoritative sources. 224pp. 9 x 12. 0-486-40150-2

Chopin, Frédéric, NOCTURNES AND POLONAISES. 20 *Nocturnes* and 11 *Polonaises* reproduced from the authoritative Mikuli edition for pianists, students, and musicologists. Commentary. 224pp. 9 x 12. 0-486-24564-0

Chopin, Frédéric, WALTZES AND SCHERZOS. All of the Scherzos and nearly all (20) of the Waltzes from the authoritative Mikuli edition. Editorial commentary. 160pp. 9 x 12. 0-486-24316-8

Cofone, Charles J. F. (ed.), ELIZABETH ROGERS HIR VIRGINALL BOOKE. All 112 pieces from noted 1656 manuscript, most never before published. Composers include Thomas Brewer, William Byrd, Orlando Gibbons, etc. Calligraphy by editor. 125pp. 9 x 12. 0-486-23138-0

Dover Piano and Keyboard Editions

Couperin, François, KEYBOARD WORKS/Series One: Ordres I–XIII; Series Two: Ordres XIV–XXVII and Miscellaneous Pieces. Over 200 pieces. Reproduced directly from edition prepared by Johannes Brahms and Friedrich Chrysander. Total of 496pp. 8⅛ x 11.
Series I: 0-486-25795-9; Series II: 0-486-25796-7

Debussy, Claude, COMPLETE PRELUDES, Books 1 and 2. 24 evocative works that reveal the essence of Debussy's genius for musical imagery, among them many of the composer's most famous piano compositions. Glossary of French terms. 128pp. 8⅜ x 11¼.   0-486-25970-6

Debussy, Claude, DEBUSSY MASTERPIECES FOR SOLO PIANO: 20 Works. From France's most innovative and influential composer–a rich compilation of works that include "Golliwogg's cakewalk," "Engulfed cathedral," "Clair de lune," and 17 others. 128pp. 9 x 12.   0-486-42425-1

Debussy, Claude, PIANO MUSIC 1888–1905. Deux Arabesques, Suite Bergamesque, Masques, first series of Images, etc. Nine others, in corrected editions. 175pp. 9⅜ x 12¼.   0-486-22771-5

Dvořák, Antonín, HUMORESQUES AND OTHER WORKS FOR SOLO PIANO. Humoresques, Op. 101, complete, Silhouettes, Op. 8, Poetic Tone Pictures, Theme with Variations, Op. 36, 4 Slavonic Dances, more. 160pp. 9 x 12.   0-486-28355-0

de Falla, Manuel, AMOR BRUJO AND EL SOMBRERO DE TRES PICOS FOR SOLO PIANO. With these two popular ballets, *El Amor Brujo* (Love, the Magician) and *El Sombrero de Tres Picos* (The Three-Cornered Hat), Falla brought the world's attention to the music of Spain. The composer himself made these arrangements of the complete ballets for piano solo. xii+132pp. 9 x 12.   0-486-44170-9

Fauré, Gabriel, COMPLETE PRELUDES, IMPROMPTUS AND VALSES-CAPRICES. Eighteen elegantly wrought piano works in authoritative editions. Only one-volume collection available. 144pp. 9 x 12. (Not available in France or Germany)   0-486-25789-4

Fauré, Gabriel, NOCTURNES AND BARCAROLLES FOR SOLO PIANO. 12 nocturnes and 12 barcarolles reprinted from authoritative French editions. 208pp. 9⅜ x 12¼. (Not available in France or Germany)
0-486-27955-3

Feofanov, Dmitry (ed.), RARE MASTERPIECES OF RUSSIAN PIANO MUSIC: Eleven Pieces by Glinka, Balakirev, Glazunov and Others. Glinka's *Prayer,* Balakirev's *Reverie,* Liapunov's *Transcendental Etude, Op. 11, No. 10,* and eight others–full, authoritative scores from Russian texts. 144pp. 9 x 12.   0-486-24659-0

Franck, César, ORGAN WORKS. Composer's best-known works for organ, including Six Pieces, Trois Pieces, and Trois Chorals. Oblong format for easy use at keyboard. Authoritative Durand edition. 208pp. 11⅜ x 8¼.
0-486-25517-4

Gottschalk, Louis M., PIANO MUSIC. 26 pieces (including covers) by early 19th-century American genius. "Bamboula," "The Banjo," other Creole, Negro-based material, through elegant salon music. 301pp. 9¼ x 12.
0-486-21683-7

Granados, Enrique, GOYESCAS, SPANISH DANCES AND OTHER WORKS FOR SOLO PIANO. Great Spanish composer's most admired, most performed suites for the piano, in definitive Spanish editions. 176pp. 9 x 12.
0-486-25481-X

Grieg, Edvard, COMPLETE LYRIC PIECES FOR PIANO. All 66 pieces from Grieg's ten sets of little mood pictures for piano, favorites of generations of pianists. 224pp. 9⅜ x 12¼.   0-486-26176-X

Handel, G. F., KEYBOARD WORKS FOR SOLO INSTRUMENTS. 35 neglected works from Handel's vast oeuvre, originally jotted down as improvisations. Includes Eight Great Suites, others. New sequence. 174pp. 9⅜ x 12¼.   0-486-24338-9

Haydn, Joseph, COMPLETE PIANO SONATAS. 52 sonatas reprinted from authoritative Breitkopf & Härtel edition. Extremely clear and readable; ample space for notes, analysis. 464pp. 9⅜ x 12¼.
Vol. I: 0-486-24726-0; Vol. II: 0-486-24727-9

Jasen, David A. (ed.), RAGTIME GEMS: Original Sheet Music for 25 Ragtime Classics. Includes original sheet music and covers for 25 rags, including three of Scott Joplin's finest: "Searchlight Rag," "Rose Leaf Rag," and "Fig Leaf Rag." 122pp. 9 x 12.   0-486-25248-5

Joplin, Scott, COMPLETE PIANO RAGS. All 38 piano rags by the acknowledged master of the form, reprinted from the publisher's original editions complete with sheet music covers. Introduction by David A. Jasen. 208pp. 9 x 12.   0-486-25807-6

Liszt, Franz, ANNÉES DE PÈLERINAGE, COMPLETE. Authoritative Russian edition of piano masterpieces: *Première Année (Suisse): Deuxième Année (Italie)* and *Venezia e Napoli; Troisième Année,* other related pieces. 288pp. 9⅜ x 12¼.   0-486-25627-8

Liszt, Franz, BEETHOVEN SYMPHONIES NOS. 6–9 TRANSCRIBED FOR SOLO PIANO. Includes Symphony No. 6 in F major, Op. 68, "Pastorale"; Symphony No. 7 in A major, Op. 92; Symphony No. 8 in F major, Op. 93; and Symphony No. 9 in D minor, Op. 125, "Choral." A memorable tribute from one musical genius to another. 224pp. 9 x 12.   0-486-41884-7

Liszt, Franz, COMPLETE ETUDES FOR SOLO PIANO, Series I: Including the Transcendental Etudes, edited by Busoni. Also includes Etude in 12 Exercises, 12 Grandes Etudes and Mazeppa. Breitkopf & Härtel edition. 272pp. 8⅜ x 11¼.   0-486-25815-7

Liszt, Franz, COMPLETE ETUDES FOR SOLO PIANO, Series II: Including the Paganini Etudes and Concert Etudes, edited by Busoni. Also includes Morceau de Salon, Ab Irato. Breitkopf & Härtel edition. 192pp. 8⅜ x 11¼.   0-486-25816-5

Liszt, Franz, COMPLETE HUNGARIAN RHAPSODIES FOR SOLO PIANO. All 19 Rhapsodies reproduced directly from authoritative Russian edition. All headings, footnotes translated to English. 224pp. 8⅜ x 11¼.
0-486-24744-9

Liszt, Franz, LISZT MASTERPIECES FOR SOLO PIANO: 13 Works. Masterworks by the supreme piano virtuoso of the 19th century: *Hungarian Rhapsody No. 2 in C-sharp minor, Consolation No. 3 in D-Flat major, Liebestraum No. 3 in A-flat major, La Campanella* (Paganini Etude No. 3), and nine others. 128pp. 9 x 12.   0-486-41379-9

Liszt, Franz, MEPHISTO WALTZ AND OTHER WORKS FOR SOLO PIANO. Rapsodie Espagnole, Liebestraüme Nos. 1–3, Valse Oubliée No. 1, Nuages Gris, Polonaises Nos. 1 and 2, Grand Galop Chromatique, more. 192pp. 8⅜ x 11¼.   0-486-28147-7

Liszt, Franz, PIANO TRANSCRIPTIONS FROM FRENCH AND ITALIAN OPERAS. Virtuoso transformations of themes by Mozart, Verdi, Bellini, other masters, into unforgettable music for piano. Published in association with American Liszt Society. 247pp. 9 x 12.   0-486-24273-0

Maitland, J. Fuller, Squire, W. B. (eds.), THE FITZWILLIAM VIRGINAL BOOK. Famous early 17th-century collection of keyboard music, 300 works by Morley, Byrd, Bull, Gibbons, etc. Modern notation. Total of 938pp. 8⅜ x 11. Two-vol. set.   0-486-21068-5, 0-486-21069-3

Medtner, Nikolai, COMPLETE FAIRY TALES FOR SOLO PIANO. Thirty-eight complex, surprising pieces by an underrated Russian 20th-century Romantic whose music is more cerebral and harmonically adventurous than Rachmaninoff's. 272pp. 9 x 12. (Available in U.S. only)
0-486-41683-6